MARK MATLOCK

WISDOM ON...
TIME AND MONEY

MARK MATLOCK

WISDOM ON...
TIME AND MONEY

Wisdom On...Time and Money
Copyright 2008 by Mark Matlock

Youth Specialties resources, 300 S. Pierce St., El Cajon, CA 92020 are published by Zondervan, 5300 Patterson Ave. SE, Grand Rapids, MI 49530.

ISBN 978-0-310-27928-0

Web site addresses listed in this book were current at the time of publication. Please contact Youth Specialties via e-mail (YS@YouthSpecialties.com) to report URLs that are no longer operational and replacement URLs if available.

Cover design by SharpSeven Design
Interior design by David Conn

Printed in the United States of America

08 09 10 11 12 • 16 15 14 13 12 11 10 9 8 7 6 5 4 3 2 1

TABLE OF CONTENTS

During the writing of this book, my eight-year-old daughter Skye was diagnosed with Type 1 diabetes. That diagnosis turned the lives of my family upside down for several months while Skye was stabilized and we as a family learned how to manage this awful intrusion into her life. I'm happy to say that as this book goes to press, she's doing well.

I couldn't have completed this volume were it not for many people who put in hours to help. We all learned a lot about "Time and Money." This book wasn't just an assembling of words; it was a learning experience.

A big thanks to my long-time friend and collaborator Chris Lyon, who jumped into the deep end to help. Also to Jay Howver and Roni Meek at Youth Specialties, who gave me great flexibility on my deadlines. And, of course, my editor Randy Southern, who had his year and work schedule altered when my deadlines shifted. I cannot thank you enough.

ACKNOWLEDGMENTS

CHAPTER 1
EASY MONEY

Have you ever wanted something really badly? In the back of my *Boy's Life* magazine, there was an ad from the Johnson Smith Company for all kinds of amazing gadgets and novelties designed to grab a boy's interest. The ad was filled with wonderful items like spy cameras, X-ray glasses, insect-eating plants, plastic dog poop, garlic-flavored chewing gum, and—best of all—magic tricks.

Man, did I love magic tricks. The ad said one trick would allow me to pull money out of the air with my bare hands. I'd seen a magician on television use the trick to fill buckets with half dollars—that was the trick I had to have! For just $1.50, plus another $1 for shipping and handling, I'd be able to make unlimited amounts of cash. I showed the ad to my father, who wasn't nearly as enthusiastic as I was.

"Mark, this is all hype," he warned. "You won't be able to make real money. It's a trick."

But I knew my father was wrong. So I counted $2.50 from my piggy bank (which literally was a pig-shaped bank), handed it to my dad, and asked him to write out a check to send in with my order.

Day after day I waited for the mail carrier to arrive. *How big would the box be? I wondered. How much money would I be able to make?* At night I dreamed of wearing a tuxedo as I stood in front of my first grade class, pulled money out of the air, and impressed all the girls with my suave performance (not to mention my money-making potential). I also dreamed of taking my family on great vacations and being asked to perform on television.

This was the life-changing event I'd been waiting for. My package couldn't arrive fast enough! Why, oh why, did I have to wait six to eight weeks for delivery?

Finally, the big day arrived. I checked the mailbox and found a box with my name on it from the Johnson Smith Company. The box was smaller than I'd expected, but that didn't faze me. I was moments away from turning my life around. I ran up to my room and opened the red, white, and blue box with the EZ-Magic logo on the front. Inside the box I found...a plastic coin. It was the size of a quarter, and there was a piece of double-stick tape on the back.

What?

I read the directions:

Step 1: Remove the backing from the double-stick tape.

Step 2: Attach the coin to the back of your thumbnail.

Step 3: With your hand palm open to the audience, reach into the air as if picking something from it; this motion will reveal the coin.

Step 4: Pretend to put it into a container in which you have already placed several coins.

Step 5: Repeat, and then pour out the coins for others to examine. Real money from the air!

Remember, practice makes perfect and shhhh! Never reveal the secret.

I threw the box against the wall. Money didn't come from the air! It was a con!

My dad used the experience to teach me a lesson that I didn't fully learn until I was much older: If something sounds too good to be true, then it probably is.

CHAPTER 2
THE WANT

Raise your hand if you've ever wanted to be fabulously wealthy—rich enough to buy anything and everything you want. Now raise your hand if you've ever wanted to be free to spend all of your time doing whatever you feel like doing.

Obviously, those are selfish dreams. And you've heard it said time and time again that money can't buy happiness and that with freedom comes responsibility. Yet that doesn't keep us from holding on to those dreams. If we ever stumble across one of those three-wish genies, we'll know what to ask for.

That desire for money—and all the sweet stuff that money buys—is part of our makeup. So is the desire to do the things we love. It's in our nature to want those things. The apostle John calls it the "lust of [the] eyes" (1 John 2:16).

That lust—that nagging want—is one aspect of "worldliness," the self-centered attitudes and focus of humankind. The Bible has much to say about that topic. However, before we start applying biblical wisdom, we need to explore the role that "want" plays in our everyday lives.

For example, how many of your decisions are driven by a desire for things or for personal freedom? Will the "lust of the eyes" influence your career decisions? How about your college choices? Will it sway your decisions regarding whom you'll date and perhaps eventually marry? Will it determine how you save or spend your time and money? These are questions that most people—even those who follow Jesus—wrestle with their entire lives. *What am I really living for? What is driving my life?*

Beyond these big philosophical questions, there are practical ones to consider as well. We all have time to spend—24 hours a day, to be exact. And most of us have at least a little money to play with. What are the wisest choices we can make with our minutes and dollars? Is it okay to spend time just goofing off? How much work is enough—and how much is too much? If I'm going to give money away, to whom should I give it? How much should I give? Is it okay to borrow money from my parents, friends, and international credit-lending corporations? Does God really care about any of this stuff?

The answer to that last question is "yup." God certainly does care about what we do with our burning "want" for money and free time. He wants us to learn how to spend, save, earn, and burn our time and money wisely.

Are you ready to find out how to do that? Let's get started.

CHAPTER 3
TIME FOR WISDOM

Self-help experts, life coaches, and various other professionals often lump together time and money within the larger category of "resource management." On the surface that seems to make sense; after all, both areas require self-control, discipline, and good planning in order to be managed successfully. However, the common ground ends there. The fact is, time and money are very different resources that require vastly different strategies for wise living.

Unlike money, which some people have a lot of and some people have little of, time is available to everyone in equal amounts. Each of us starts the day with the same number of hours. And each of us ends the day having spent all of those hours doing something. What's more, we can't save time as we do money. We can't say, "I'm going to spend only 12 hours living today so I can have 36 hours to spend tomorrow."

Time passes whether we like it or not, whether we use it or not, whether we're sleeping or sick or productive or playing. We can't borrow it, capture it, speed it up, or slow it down. It's a constant and limited resource.

Someone once asked, "Why doesn't God just take us all to heaven the moment we're born again into his family? Our sins are forgiven, right? He knows we'll eventually be with him forever in heaven. What is he waiting for? What's the point of all this *time* we have to wade through between now and when we get to heaven?"

It's an excellent question, and it's one worth thinking about. I love the way Charlie Peacock answered it in his song "The Secret of Time":

> Time is a gift of love and grace
>
> Without time there'd be no time to change

Time to be tried, humbled and broken

Time to hear the word of love spoken

In other words, God gives us the time prior to eternity to grow closer to being the person we're meant to be in Jesus. Becoming like Christ—becoming spiritually mature—involves learning to trust God more and more. And that process takes time—days, months, years, decades.

So the key is, we must be willing to use our time for that purpose. How many of us actually use our time looking for ways to be "tried, humbled and broken" so we can "hear the word of love spoken"? Not many. Instead, most of us (including me) burn time looking for ways to avoid being tried, humbled, broken, and needy for God's love.

God exists outside of time, of course. That's what the word *eternal* means. God doesn't experience the passing of minutes and hours and days. That's why Scripture says that for him a day is like a thousand years and vice versa (see 2 Peter 3:8).

God can reach into time at any moment he wishes and impact our lives in any way he wishes. We call that control over time and the universe God's sovereignty, and it's just one of the countless things that make him awesome.

By comparison, we are slaves to the always-ticking clock and the always-flipping calendar. Our destiny is to live and die in a relatively small number of years—a tiny percentage of human history. That makes us very, very small. Terrifyingly puny. We can never escape time on this side of heaven.

So what should we do with the limited time we have? What's worth doing when our lives race by at lightning speed and end in a poof? Moses thought a lot about that very question. In fact, it seemed to bother him. If you read Psalm 90, the only psalm in the Bible that's attributed to him, you'll see what I mean. Here's a bit of it:

Teach us to number our days aright,
that we may gain a heart of wisdom.

Relent, O Lord! How long will it be?
Have compassion on your servants.

Satisfy us in the morning with your unfailing love,
that we may sing for joy and be glad all our days.

Make us glad for as many days as you have afflicted us,
for as many years as we have seen trouble.

May your deeds be shown to your servants,
your splendor to their children.

May the favor of the Lord our God rest upon us;

establish the work of our hands for us—yes, establish the work of our hands. (Psalm 90:12-17)

When Moses thought about how little time any of us has in this life, he asked for several things. The first thing he requested is that God would help us make the best possible use of our time. Moses realized that a life that matters is made up of lots of days that matter. If we make the best possible use of our time, Moses realized, then we'll gain wise hearts. *Lord, help everyone who's reading this book to gain wise hearts to make the best use of his or her short time in this life.*

Next, Moses asked God to help us avoid wasting our time being dissatisfied with life and choose to be satisfied with his love. In fact, Moses wanted us to be so satisfied that we'd spend all of our troubling days singing for joy and being glad. Are *you* listening to hear the word of love spoken?

Third, Moses prayed that we'd see God's continuing work in the world around us. *Show those of us who are stuck here in time, Lord, that you're out there doing amazing things. Help us to see it.* Are you looking for God's splendorous deeds?

Finally, Moses begged God to establish the work of our hands. He wanted us to make sure that our time on this earth wouldn't be wasted doing worthless things that won't matter in a hundred years. *Establish the works of our hands, Father; please do us that favor.*

Why don't you make Moses' prayer your own? Remember, to fear God's awesome power and to ask for his help is to begin the journey toward wisdom. Don't forget that your time here on earth is in God's outside-of-time hands.

SELF-EVALUATION: HEART, HEAD, TIME

COLOSSIANS 3:1-3 SAYS THIS:

Since, then, you have been raised with Christ, set your hearts on things above, where Christ is seated at the right hand of God. Set your minds on things above, not on earthly things. For you died, and your life is now hidden with Christ in God.

Summary: God says your life—the one that will always matter—exists right now in heaven with Jesus. So he tells us to set our emotions and thoughts on heavenly things.

Ask yourself:

· What percentage of your time do you have your *heart* (or emotions)

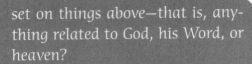

set on things above—that is, anything related to God, his Word, or heaven?

· What percentage of your time do you have your *mind* set on things above?

· How would your daily routine—the way you spend your time—change if you spent more time with your heart and mind focused on heavenly things?

CHAPTER 4

WHAT TIME IS IT?

I heard a story about a man who learned his father had just died. The man reacted to the news in a rather unusual way. He tried to ignore it—to pretend it didn't happen. Why? He wanted to be in a productive, joyful season. He wanted his life during that time to be about good things. He didn't want his time to be about loss and sadness and grieving. Try as he might, though, he couldn't make his plan work. He couldn't postpone his grief. He eventually had to break down and submit to the season he was in.

King David knew what he was talking about when he told God: "My times are in your hands" (Psalm 31:15). We don't control our times. We have little say over the season of life we live in or how long it lasts. David's son Solomon used every bit of his God-given wisdom when he wrote these words in Ecclesiastes 3:1-8—

There is a time for everything,
and a season for every activity under heaven:

a time to be born and a time to die,
a time to plant and a time to uproot,

a time to kill and a time to heal,
a time to tear down and a time to build,

a time to weep and a time to laugh,
a time to mourn and a time to dance,

a time to scatter stones and a time to gather them,
a time to embrace and a time to refrain,

a time to search and a time to give up,
a time to keep and a time to throw away,

a time to tear and a time to mend,
a time to be silent and a time to speak,

a time to love and a time to hate,
a time for war and a time for peace.

An essential element in using our time wisely is recognizing the season in which God has placed us and embracing it. For example, a person shouldn't expect life to be full of wild celebrations in a season of mourning. On the flip side, it's a shame when people miss a season of good times because they're too busy thinking about all the sad things in life.

If you're an unmarried person, God's Word says you should view your present life as a season to "refrain from embracing" (having sex). Then when you become a newlywed, it's time to enjoy your season of "embracing."

We must all submit to the God who determines our times. Our moments are in his hands. It's pointless to say, "I will reject God because this is not a season of laughing or dancing or peace or building." The only wise option is to ask God to help us live wisely in whatever season we find ourselves—to help us make the most of it—because soon enough it will pass, and then we'll find ourselves in a different season.

SELF-EVALUATION

Ask yourself: What season am I in right now? Read through Ecclesiastes 3:1-8 again. Which of those times best describes your current circumstances?

Now that you've identified your season, ask God to help you understand how to live wisely in that time. Ask him to help you recognize your personal season and make the most of your hours and days for as long as your life lasts.

CHAPTER 5
TIME TYCOONS

Like money, time can be invested. In fact, we all invest our minutes and days in very specific things. Sometimes we invest our hours in worthless ventures. Other times, we invest them in things that prove hugely profitable in the long run. The question is, does it matter to God what kind of a return we get on our investment of time?

(Hint: Yes!)

In the Bible passage that we usually call the Parable of the Talents, Jesus appears to be talking about money. (A "talent" was a unit of money.) However, the principle of this parable can also be applied to how we invest our time.

Here's the story from Matthew 25:14-30:

> "Again, it will be like a man going on a journey, who called his servants

and entrusted his property to them. To one he gave five talents of money, to another two talents, and to another one talent, each according to his ability. Then he went on his journey. The man who had received the five talents went at once and put his money to work and gained five more. So also, the one with the two talents gained two more. But the man who had received the one talent went off, dug a hole in the ground and hid his master's money.

"After a long time the master of those servants returned and settled accounts with them. The man who had received the five talents brought the other five. 'Master,' he said, 'you entrusted me with five talents. See, I have gained five more.'

"His master replied, 'Well done, good and faithful servant! You have been faithful with a few things; I will put

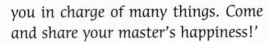

you in charge of many things. Come and share your master's happiness!'

"The man with the two talents also came. 'Master,' he said, 'you entrusted me with two talents; see, I have gained two more.'

"His master replied, 'Well done, good and faithful servant! You have been faithful with a few things; I will put you in charge of many things. Come and share your master's happiness!'

"Then the man who had received the one talent came. 'Master,' he said, 'I knew that you are a hard man, harvesting where you have not sown and gathering where you have not scattered seed. So I was afraid and went out and hid your talent in the ground. See, here is what belongs to you.'

"His master replied, 'You wicked, lazy servant! So you knew that I harvest where I have not sown and gather where I have not scattered seed? Well then, you should have put my money on deposit with the bankers, so that when I returned I would have received it back with interest.

" 'Take the talent from him and give it to the one who has the ten talents. For everyone who has will be given more, and he will have an abundance. Whoever does not have, even what he has will be taken from him. And throw that worthless servant outside, into the darkness, where there will be weeping and gnashing of teeth.' "

Yikes! The guy who took the money and buried it—just to be safe—got scorched by his master. Instead of putting the money into play by working hard and taking risks like the other servants did, he went the easy route. He buried what he'd been given. He thought all his master would care about was his not losing the money on something worthless. But the master made it clear that he expected his servants to get in the game, to find a way to make the money grow, to do something worthwhile with it.

We talk a lot about money in the rest of this book, so I'm going to connect this parable to how we use our time. All of us receive time from God. As Christians, we're called to use that time to follow Jesus, to make the most of our lives by sacrificing them in serving him.

Anything worthwhile in life requires an investment of time. Think of any person you admire. Musicians—the good ones—invest thousands of hours with their instruments. Artists dedicate years to developing their craft, their style, their approach to their art. Successful business people put in long days to establish their trade, to understand their product and their customers, and to figure out a marketing approach that will bring the two together. Great athletes aren't handed sneaker contracts just for graduating from college. Even those who are gifted with lots of natural talent hone that talent through grueling hours on the road, in the weight room, and in practice.

To be great at anything in life takes lots and lots of focused time—including being a follower of Jesus. Highly productive disciples of Jesus aren't just born (again) successful. Real difference-makers in the body of Christ use the same finite amount of time we're all given to read and understand God's Word. They put in hour after hour in the "weight room" of personal prayer and worship. And they come together for "practice" with other believers every week, to work out what it really means to be a follower of Jesus.

How are you investing the time God has given you in order to make a return for his "company"? Are you in the game, putting in the hours, taking risks by trying new things, looking for new ways to become more like Jesus? Or have you buried your gift of time under hours and hours of entertainment, meaningless conversations, and simple distractions?

What's your plan for creating a life that matters? In order to answer that question, you'll have to decide what you're going to do with your time.

SELF-EVALUATION: WHERE'D THE TIME GO?
On a sheet of paper, make a list of the following items:

SLEEPING
EATING
GOING TO SCHOOL
STUDYING
PRACTICING AND PLAYING SPORTS

GOING TO CHURCH AND YOUTH GROUP
READING THE BIBLE/PRAYING/MINIS-
TERING TO OTHERS
WORKING FOR MONEY
DOING CHORES
HANGING WITH FRIENDS/TALKING ON
THE PHONE/INSTANT MESSAGING
ENTERTAINING YOURSELF (WATCHING
TV AND MOVIES, PLAYING VIDEO
GAMES, LISTENING TO MUSIC, SURFING
THE WEB, READING)
DOING NOTHING
OTHER

Every week contains 168 hours. Next to each item on the list, estimate how many hours you spend doing that activity.

After you've finished your estimates, get a pocket-sized notebook and start an actual log of your activities. Write down every activity that occupies your time over the next seven days. You might want to round off each entry to the nearest quarter hour. For instance, if it takes you about an hour and 15 minutes to get ready for school, write down 1.25 HOURS.

At the end of your week, add up all the numbers. The total should come to about 168. Now compare your first list of estimated times with your second list of actual times spent living your life.

THINK ABOUT:

· Do I notice any areas in which I'm spending too much time doing things that aren't worth that many hours?

· What items on the list need more of my time and attention?

· What specific steps could I take to make sure I'm investing my time in a life that really matters?

THINK AHEAD:

· Have I been too busy with other areas of my life to spend time with God in his Word and in prayer?

· Do I have time to hang with friends so I can encourage them—and be encouraged by them?

· Am I investing enough time in getting worthwhile things done?

CHAPTER 6
MARY VERSUS MARTHA

It was a huge day for sisters Mary and Martha. Their house was jammed with visitors. Of course that was to be expected—Jesus had come for dinner, and he always traveled with a crowd. That meant a lot of work for his hosts—for *one* of them, at least.

While Martha scurried around the house trying to make everything just right, her sister Mary sat at Jesus' feet, listening to him talk. *What's she thinking?* Martha must have wondered. *After all, this is her house, too. She should be helping me!*

Finally, Martha couldn't take it anymore. Since Jesus was the only person Mary listened to, Martha presented her case to him:

> "Lord, don't you care that my sister has left me to do the work by myself? Tell her to help me!"

"Martha, Martha," the Lord answered, "you are worried and upset about many things, but only one thing is needed. Mary has chosen what is better, and it will not be taken away from her." (Luke 10:40-42)

There's a huge clue to be found in this story about how we should spend our time. Yes, it's good to be busy doing worthwhile things. And what could be more worthwhile than volunteering your home and your time in support of Jesus' teaching ministry? You could argue that given her place in the world and her status as an influential woman, Martha made the best possible use of her time and money resources in that particular season of her life. By preparing her home for Jesus, she was doing a good thing—a really good thing!

Obviously her task required a lot of work. It involved tending to many details. All of the people who hung out with Jesus needed to be fed and re-freshed. They basically lived on the road, after all. All kinds of prepara-tions needed to be made. With so much to be done, it's no wonder this question occurred to Martha: *Is it fair for Mary to ignore the things that need to be done and just sit at Jesus' feet?*

Yet there's another, more important question that didn't occur to Martha: *Which is better—putting my hospitality skills to use for Jesus' sake (a good thing) or sitting at his feet and actually listen-ing to what he has to say?* What would you have done in Martha's situation? Would you have chosen the *good* op-tion or the better and potentially *life-changing* one?

I know many solid, performance-ori-ented, and achieving Christian stu-dents who are so busy doing things for God—and for everyone else in their lives—that they have no time to listen to the words of Jesus, to meditate on what he wants from them, or to talk to him (that is, talk to him when they're not in a car or on the run).

As you look at your busy schedule, can you find some blocks of time to set aside for hearing the Master? If not, you might need to make some room by using perhaps the most difficult two-letter word in the English language: No.

Saying no is a lifelong struggle for those of us who are "pleasers" and who love to do really good things. However, Jesus taught us that the wise use of our time includes plenty of hours spent alone with him. A healthy, God-honoring schedule also includes plenty of time for sleep, exercise, eating right, and playing (yes, playing!). You can skip those things for only so long before you start to feel the effects.

That's where the difficult two-letter solution comes in. Practice it with me: No. No. NO! "No, thank you." "Sorry, I can't make it." "Oh, I'd love to help with that project, but I'm out of room in my schedule." "I can't help you, but I know someone who might be able to."

If it's just too painful for you to tell people no, then do what a couple of my student friends have done. They've talked their parents into playing the bad guys for them. When someone asks them to do something, they say, "I'll have to ask my mom." Then later they can say, "My mom says I've got too much going on to take that project. Sorry."

I understand that some seasons are busier than others. It's not unusual to have a few weeks here or there when it's tough to find time to spend in the Word or in prayer—or even in bed sleeping. But if you're waking up to the fact that your whole life is always so full that you just laugh when someone asks how much sleep you got last night, then it's time to "go negative."

So would you please read the rest of this book—*right now?* I think that would be best. Oh, you can't? You don't have time? I understand. (*Very good!*)

CHAPTER 7
SLOTH BUSTING

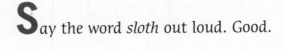

Say the word *sloth* out loud. Good.

Now say it really, really slowly. S-s-s-l-o-o-o-o-th. The word reminds me of the way Jabba the Hut (of *Star Wars* fame) talks, all slow and slimy. It's one of those words that sounds as ugly as its meaning. I used to think of sloth as laziness times 10, but it's much worse than that. **After all, sloth is on the list of seven deadly sins.**

Some translations of the Bible call a slothful person a "sluggard." Whatever term you use for it, sloth is the opposite of spending time wisely. Here's what the writer of Proverbs said about it:

> The sluggard says, "There is a lion in the road, a fierce lion roaming the streets!"

> As a door turns on its hinges, so a sluggard turns on his bed.

The sluggard buries his hand in the dish; he is too lazy to bring it back to his mouth.

The sluggard is wiser in his own eyes than seven men who answer discreetly. (Proverbs 26:13-16)

In modern terms he's talking about that feeling you get when you've been watching TV for hours and all the while you're sinking lower and lower into the couch cushions, when even the *thought* of moving is painful, and when you don't have the energy to find the remote and change the channel.

It's one thing to have that experience once in a while, but some people dedicate their lives to sloth. And that has a lot to do with dedicating one's self to TV. And DVDs. And video games. And more TV. And a microwave cheese dog. And another video game.

Neil Postman, in his great book *Amusing Ourselves to Death* (Penguin, 1986), said that part of the problem with television is that it creates the illusion that we're doing something when we're not. Someone with a camera went on a safari in Africa, so I fool myself into thinking I've also had a little bit of that experience because I watched a show about it. In reality, the only "experience" I had was sitting on my couch.

A similar thing happens with video games. "I conquered five levels of *Halo 2!*" Well, yes and no. Actually, I moved my thumbs and forefingers a lot for, like, 16 hours. But that's the only thing that happened in the real world. Except for bathroom breaks. And that cheese dog.

Sloth is an abuse of God's gift of time to us. There's nothing wrong with watching TV or playing video games occasionally. (I'm not so sure about those cheese dogs.) But we've got to be wise enough—and honest enough with ourselves—to notice when watching and playing has become the most important, most meaningful, and most exciting parts of our lives. That should tell us that we've arrived in the neighborhood of slothiness.

The trouble with a sloth habit is that it's like quicksand. The longer you stay, the harder it is to break free. You might need to recruit some friends to pull you back into the real world where you can spend your time chasing a life that matters with your real legs and looking for God's greatness with your own eyes—instead of through someone else's camera lens.

The Bible is full of God's instructions to turn sloth into diligence, hard work, and creative expression. The writer of Hebrews urged his Christian readers not to become lazy Christians:

We want each of you to show this

same diligence to the very end, in order to make your hope sure. We do not want you to become lazy, but to imitate those who through faith and patience inherit what has been promised. (Hebrews 6:11-12)

SELF-EVALUATION: SLOTH OLYMPICS

Think about your five closest friends outside of your family. Ask yourself: *Which of these friends is closest to slipping into sloth? Who spends the most hours in front of video screens?*

If it's you, why not call your least slothful friend and ask him or her to come over and help you get out of your quicksand? If it's someone else, ask God to help you help that person get involved in some real-life activities that are worth the gift of time we've all received from God.

CHAPTER 8

LIVING FOR MONEY
DOESN'T PAY

If you believe recent statistics, American students care more about money now than ever before. The U.S. Census Bureau regularly interviews incoming college freshmen about a variety of topics, then tracks any changes in their answers over time. When asked for their number one priority back in groovy 1970, 79 percent of students responded that they hoped to develop a "meaningful philosophy of life." In 2005—just 35 years later—75 percent selected the option of becoming "very well-off financially" as their first goal! That's a major shift in national priorities.

That doesn't necessarily mean today's students are all selfish ogres who are out to line their pockets and rule the world. The stats could be misleading, depending on how the question was presented or which demographic was targeted. (Perhaps the survey takers hit the business college and skipped the

English department.) Or perhaps today's students are simply a little more honest than previous generations.

It's also possible that the young people of this generation have watched their parents hunt for that "meaningful philosophy of life" and come up empty-handed. They've seen families stressed out by huge debt, marriages broken up by money conflicts, and people who lived for "noble philosophies" but ended up disillusioned and discouraged. It might be more than just selfishness that motivates us to check the box that says, "I want money—and lots of it—thankyouverymuch."

Whatever the reason, though, the *fact* that 75 percent of college frosh believe that money is the best possible goal to chase in life is a huge problem. It's a monumental disaster. It's a dark omen for the future of our nation. (Does this sound like the book jacket for a Stephen King novel?)

Some people—maybe those in the economics department—might argue the opposite, claiming that the quest for money is the best possible news for the future of the world. After all, capitalism runs on our desire for wealth. If we want riches, we work harder and come up with better ways of doing things. If we all do that, we make more money, the economy grows, and people are taken care of. If nobody wanted to get rich, then the economy might just fall apart, right?

If you keep reading this book, you'll see that I'm a good capitalist. I believe in hard work, good business, and even building wealth. (Really.) I believe that making, saving, giving, and spending money wisely usually results in people having more money. And that's a good thing. So why am I freaking out about three quarters of all incoming college students listing "having plenty o' the green" as Job One?

Money may be a great thing to have; but it's an evil, stupid, and pointless thing to live for. It's a fine thing to use, to plan for, and to be smart with; but it's a lousy reason to get out of bed in the morning.

Living for money doesn't pay off in the end. It doesn't work. Listen to Solomon, arguably the richest person who ever lived. He said the problem with the race for money is that there's no finish line:

> Whoever loves money never has money enough; whoever loves wealth is never satisfied with his income." (Ecclesiastes 5:10)

Living for money is like playing Monopoly with a limitless supply of fake cash. The game never ends. It's exciting at first when you're building your hotels and charging outrageous rental fees to your little brother every time he lands on Park Place. But if nobody ever wins and the game goes on for 10 weeks, who still cares? Where's the satisfaction?

Part of the problem, according to Solomon, is that people who live for money always end up dead in the end—just like the rest of us. But at the end of their lives, when they realize the money chase has brought them no happiness, they get ticked off:

> Naked a man comes from his mother's womb, and as he comes, so he departs. He takes nothing from his labor that he can carry in his hand.
>
> This too is a grievous evil: As a man comes, so he departs, and what does he gain, since he toils for the wind? All his days he eats in darkness, with

great frustration, affliction and anger. (Ecclesiastes 5:15-17)

But that's just one dead guy's opinion, right? I mean, it's true because it's written in the Bible, of course. But maybe we're different. Maybe money really *would* make us happy. Maybe there's some magic dollar amount that would be enough to finally scratch our money itch once and for all.

Again, the stats say, "not so much." According to research reported in London School of Economics economist Richard Layard's book *Happiness* (Penguin, 2005), self-reported levels of happiness stop climbing after income reaches about $20,000 per head. In other words, beyond getting all of our basic needs met, humans don't get happier when they get more cash.

Still, we all hold on to the stubborn idea that if we could just get "more" money, we'd have "enough" money. It's an attitude we must find a way to break—before we waste precious time chasing a goal that can't possibly pay off in the end.

According to the apostle Paul, if you have your basic needs met—meaning food, clothes, and shelter—you can have contentment. Paul agreed with Solomon in his belief that if you can't find contentment in this very moment with God, then no amount of money, no material possessions, and no other circumstance will ever make you more content.

Let me say that one more time: If you can't be content right now—in this moment—then you'll never find contentment by having more money or more stuff. Contentment is the sense that "this moment is good enough." Paul says we find it when we're living for the right thing—to serve and please God:

But godliness with contentment is great gain. For we brought nothing into the world, and we can take nothing out of it. But if we have food and clothing, we will be content with that (1 Timothy 6:6-8).

SELF-EVALUATION: MONEY LOVER?
This is a biggie. Look inside your heart—right there past the left ventricle. Ask yourself: *Where's the needle pointing on my "Money Lover Gauge"? Is it Low? Medium? High?*

After reading this chapter, what do you think it will cost you to live for money for the rest of your life? What do you think it will cost you *not* to live for money? Be honest with yourself. Then ask God to give you real wisdom about living for money.

CHAPTER 9

LIVING FOR MONEY
HURTS...EVERYONE

People who live for money never find great happiness. Even if they strike it rich, they discover wealth is not the path to contentment. So if the thing you spend your life chasing doesn't bring money or happiness, what's the point of chasing it?

That line of questioning certainly makes sense. However, if you're like me, then you probably need more reasons not to live for wealth. Sure, we can accept the idea that money can't buy happiness and contentment. But it can't hurt us to have a lot of money, right?

Right?

Well, you might be surprised.

Ed Ugel used to work in the lottery industry. He worked for a company that paid huge sums to lottery winners who elected to receive their winnings in annual payments. In his book *Money for Nothing: One Man's Journey through the Dark Side of Lottery Millions* (Collins, 2007), he describes from personal experience how he learned that the vast majority of lottery winners wish they'd never won.

Did you catch that? Most people who win the lottery eventually *regret* having purchased the ticket in the first place. It's hard to believe, but it's true. In my book, *Living a Life That Matters* (Zondervan/Youth Specialties, 2005), which deals with Solomon's search for meaning in life, I quoted a few such winners:

> "I wish all of this never would have happened. I wish I would have torn the ticket up," said Jewell Whittaker of her lottery experience after she and her husband Jack won a $113 million lump sum payout on Christmas Day 2002.

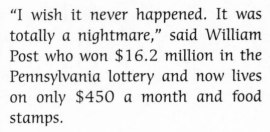

"I wish it never happened. It was totally a nightmare," said William Post who won $16.2 million in the Pennsylvania lottery and now lives on only $450 a month and food stamps.

"Winning the lottery isn't always what it's cracked up to be," said Evelyn Adams who won the New Jersey lottery twice and now lives in a trailer.

Suzanne Williams won $4.2 million in the Virginia lottery in 1993, and she is now deeper in debt than she was before she won.

So what's the problem? Why do so many lottery winners end up hating life? Susan Bradley, who founded a company called the Sudden Money Institute, says part of the problem is that people who win the lottery or suddenly inherit millions of dollars believe the same lie many of us do.

"In our culture, there is a widely held belief that money solves problems. People think if they had more money, their troubles would be over. When a family receives sudden money, they frequently learn that money can cause as many problems as it solves."

The apostle Paul put it this way:

> People who want to get rich fall into temptation and a trap and into many foolish and harmful desires that plunge men into ruin and destruction. For the love of money is a root of all kinds of evil. Some people, eager for money, have wandered from the faith and pierced themselves with many griefs. (1 Timothy 6:9-10)

Ouch. There it is. "Those who want to get rich." That's all of us, on some level. We all *want* to get rich. But the question we must ask ourselves is this: *Have I made the selfish desire to be rich such a high priority in my life that it's driving the choices I make? Am I going to become someone who lives for money?*

If so, God's Word promises that I will fall into traps, into pain, and into ruin. What if Paul's words were printed on the back of every lottery ticket or on a big plaque at the entrance to the mall or on the covers of college recruiting catalogs? How many of us would think twice before continuing our quest for money and the things it buys? How many of us would stop dreaming of "enough" wealth to get whatever we wanted?

You might be saying, "Hey, wait a minute. There's nothing wrong with going to the mall or going to college." I agree. Paul's point is that our motive is the key. The *love* of money is the root of all kinds of evil. Paul is forcing us to examine the reasons for the choices we make.

To be honest, a trip to the mall occasionally makes me wish I were rich. I start to love money a little more when I'm in that environment because I make a list of things that look good to me, things that I think would make me really happy. And I realize I'd need much more money than I currently have in order to get all of them.

Here's an even harder one: Some of you are making choices about colleges and majors and careers. So you have to ask yourself: *Am I looking for something that will make me rich? Am I angling toward an area of study in order to set myself up for life—financially speaking?* Consider this—what's the point of a college education? Is it to help you live a life that matters? If so, then making financial rewards your only criterion will lead to pain in the long run. (Remember, that's the Bible talking, not me.)

Living for money doesn't bring happiness; it brings misery and ruin. All of us have to wrestle with the question of what we're living for in order to make sure we avoid such an end.

SCENARIO: TWO BOSSES

Jared's got a problem. He got what he thought was a great summer job working for a busy lawn service with accounts all over town. He gets to drive a truck and supervise a couple of middle school guys when he goes to clients' houses. The pay is better than anything he could find working at a fast-food place or at the mall. And he gets to be outside all summer. If only his bosses could make up their minds about who is in charge, it would be a perfect job.

Jared was hired by Mr. Peters. He's an older guy who owns the business and also works for an insurance agency in town. Jared's supervisor is Mark, Mr. Peters' son. Mark tells Jared where to go each day and how to do the job. Jared really likes Mark, and Mark gives Jared a lot of freedom.

The problem is Mr. Peters and his son don't get along. Mr. Peters often stops by the shop during lunch and asks Jared to go to the house of a client who called just that morning. Then Mark tells Jared to stick to the original schedule. "New clients have to wait their turn," he says. Jared likes Mark better, but Mr. Peters signs his checks.

Jared is starting to really resent Mr. Peters. It's getting to the point where Jared almost hates to see Mr. Peters because Jared knows he'll have to choose between doing something Mark's way or doing it Mark's dad's way—or doing it *both* ways and killing himself in the process.

THINK ABOUT:

· What would you do if you were in Jared's shoes?

· Why is it so much harder to work for two bosses?

· Have you ever had to work for two bosses at the same time?

· How did that turn out?

THINK AHEAD:

· If you had to choose, which would you say is your real "boss"—living for money, living to follow Jesus, or trying to live for both?

· How does your answer change the way you think about life?

· How does it change your everyday choices? Your major life choices?

· How does it change your ability to feel content?

CHAPTER 10
YOU'VE GOT TO CHOOSE

I know many people who've been stuck between "two bosses" in one way or another. They always end up liking one of them better; and they usually try to please that one, even though they can't totally ignore the other one. It's maddening. Serving both takes extra time and energy, and it eventually leads to relationship-ending conflicts.

As a result, the person with two bosses always feels torn and often doesn't do a very good job for either employer. His whole working life turns into a frustrating mess.

Jesus said a surprising thing about money in Luke 16:13—

No servant can serve two masters. Either he will hate the one and love the other, or he will be devoted to the one and despise the other. You can't serve both God and Money.

Jared, from the illustration in the last chapter, might survive the summer by walking the line between Mr. Peters and his son, but Jesus said we *can't* serve both God and money. We always have to choose between the two. If living for God drives our lives, then we'll end up making different decisions than we would if living for money were the basis for our choices.

I know many people who started chasing both God and money at the same time. Of course, that's probably not the way they'd put it. Most would probably say, "I'm all about following God with my whole life," while thinking in the back of their minds, *And I'd really like to make some decent money while I'm following him.*

That dual pursuit may seem like it works—for a while, at least. But Jesus said we'll eventually have to choose sides. One day my love for Jesus will have to do battle with my love for money (and the stuff money buys). That's when things can get emotional. If I haven't fully committed to one or the other, Jesus said I'll end up getting mad at the one that's not my real priority. In fact he said I'll "despise" it (even while I pretend everything is fine).

From Jesus' point of view, it's not enough to choose to be a Christian and then go on with the rest of your life as you see fit. Those of us who follow him have to give up all of our other "masters." We have to make a declaration in our hearts to let go of our commitment to a minimum standard of financial success, among other things. That can be a hard declaration to make—and an even harder one to stick to.

Some people are honest enough to come right out and choose against Jesus. They want the money, and they're not willing to compromise. Pastor Ray

Steadman once read a letter to his con-
gregation that was written by the wife
of a man who had done just that:

> My husband is getting rather fed
> up with church. He is from a very
> strong Christian family, and [he]
> was a strong Christian himself.
> But now he says to get ahead in
> the world and make the kind of
> money he wants to make, you
> can't be a full-time Christian be-
> cause you either give up all you've
> got to follow Christ's claims, or
> you're not worthy. Since he's not
> worthy, why go halfway? I can't
> make him see otherwise.

Strange as it may seem, I actually admire the guy's honesty. I'm also very
sad for him. He understood what Jesus was asking way more than many
Christians I know. When he heard that
Jesus said we'd have to choose between
making him our master and making

money our master, this man made a real choice. Many of us keep trying to do both, but the path of the Master and the path of money will eventually drift too far apart for us to travel both at the same time.

I anticipate that some people who read this chapter will mock the idea of choosing between following God and chasing riches. Some of the people who were listening when Jesus first made the statement mocked it as well:

> The Pharisees, who loved money, heard all this and were sneering at Jesus. He said to them, "You are the ones who justify yourselves in the eyes of men, but God knows your hearts. What is highly valued among men is detestable in God's sight." (Luke 16:14-15)

The Pharisees were the most religious guys in town. Everyone knew it. They had both the status of being respected for their "holiness" and considerable wealth. But God knew what really mattered was in their hearts, and he detested what they valued. He hated their money-love. He knew the Pharisees weren't serving him.

When you go to college—and if you plan to graduate—you'll eventually have to declare a major. You have to choose between business or history or pre-med or library science. It's a tough choice for a lot of people to make, but you can't move on until you've made it. Jesus said the same thing about choosing between living for money and living for God.

Are you ready to make your declaration? Do you want to graduate from life with a degree in chasing riches? Or do you want to graduate with a degree that says you spent your life following Jesus no matter how much (or how little) ended up in your bank account? Which choice will matter more to you in the long run?

CHAPTER 11
WISDOM FOR WEALTH

Do you think you have to be smart to have a solid financial footing? As it turns out, you don't. According to a study from Ohio State University, people with higher I.Q. scores don't necessarily have any more money in the bank than those of us with merely average brains.

That might not be all that surprising to you, but here's where it gets interesting: High I.Q. types *do* tend to make more money from year to year; they just don't end up with any more money in the bank. That should tell us something— having money or building wealth isn't about being rich or lucky or somehow connected. And it's not about being smarter than the next person, either.

It's about being *wise*.

Intelligence and wisdom aren't the same thing. *Intelligence* is what we usually call "smarts." It's the ability to do well on a test or in school, to remember things and make connections. Being *wise* is being able to take what you know and make the best choices with that knowledge. I know plenty of people who didn't graduate near the top of their class in school, but they have gallons of wisdom about how to earn, save, give, and live with money. (What's more, I know a lot of smart guys who are broke.)

Just to be annoyingly redundant, I'll say it again: Making money is a stupid thing to live for. But everyone has to live with money. Everyone has to figure out how to make good money choices and avoid bad ones. People who make wise choices with money usually end up with more of it than those who make foolish choices. That's a benefit of wisdom.

Is having money—even lots of it—sinful? NO! Of *course* not. God blessed many of his faithful followers in the Bible with great wealth, for their own good and for the good of others. On the other hand, many followers—who were just as faithful to God—lived in near poverty or off the gifts of generous friends for most of their lives. The amount of money that comes our way is *not* an indication of how much God loves us.

Once more: The amount of money that comes to us is *not* a sign of God's favor in our lives. It's not an indication of how sinful we are or aren't. It's not more spiritual to be rich, and it's not more spiritual to be broke. God promises to provide what we need when we need it.

Having said that, the amount of money we *keep* does sometimes relate to how *wise* we are. In almost all cases, establishing wealth has far more to do with learning how to keep and grow money over time than it does with "striking it rich."

God always wants us to live wisely—in every area of our lives. James tells us that God is standing by right this second, just waiting to give wisdom to anyone who asks for it—and who really believes God is the best source for it (see James 1:5-8).

In Proverbs 4:5-7, Solomon begs his young readers to get wisdom:

> Get wisdom, get understanding; do not forget my words or swerve from them. Do not forsake wisdom, and she will protect you; love her, and she will watch over you. Wisdom is supreme; therefore get wisdom. Though it cost all you have, get understanding.

Notice what Solomon—the richest guy ever—did *not* say there. He didn't say, "Get money! Money will protect you! Money is supreme!" No, Solomon said the most valuable resource you can acquire is wisdom. In fact, he said that even if it costs everything you have, wisdom is worth it.

Remember, in addition to being uber-rich, Solomon was also the wisest guy ever. When God told Solomon in a dream that he would give Solomon anything he asked, Solomon asked for wisdom. After all, he had a whole kingdom to run, and he wanted to make sure he did it right. Then God said he'd make Solomon the wisest man ever. So we can trust that King Solomon knew what he was talking about when he shouted, "Get wisdom!"

We've already seen that financial wisdom starts with not living for money. In the following sections, we'll look at some of the Bible's teachings about how to be wise with the money God allows us to earn or receive.

CHAPTER 12
WORK LIKE IT MATTERS

One day while I was visiting a church as a guest speaker at a youth conference, I saw a student pull up in a nice four-by-four truck loaded with options. It was beautiful. I jokingly wondered aloud if the teenage driver was spoiled by his parents. The youth leader quickly set me straight about Brad. He told me this high-schooler had built up a very successful business of his own, and he'd bought the truck with his own money. My jaw dropped.

As a younger teen, Brad opted to spend his summer break helping build a house to earn some cash, while most of his friends chose to take the summer off. The following summer, Brad received the financing to build another house—one of his own. He served as the contractor on the project, doing much of the work himself and using the skills he'd learned the year before. At the end of that summer, he sold the house for a good profit.

The next year Brad arranged financing for the construction of *three* houses. Again, he sold them at the end of the summer—each for a profit. By using financial wisdom—and the willingness to work smart and work hard—this teenager built some honest wealth for himself. The youth leader then told me that Brad was generously paying for half of the youth group's upcoming summer mission trip.

I wouldn't expect many teenagers to be able to pull off that kind of working success so early in life. But everyone can practice the principles of working wisely.

We can't talk about time and money without talking about work. We all know that paying work involves trading a limited resource—your time—for money. Your time is all yours. You own it (or as much of it as your parents allow you to own). It's yours to spend on rest, relaxation, or fun. But it's also yours to trade or sell or use to make money for yourself. When you trade your time (and effort) for money, that's work.

Most students (and adults) I know sometimes resent having to work—that's normal. But the wisdom of God's Word urges us to work as though our work matters—even if that work is writing school papers, chasing toddlers, or restocking store shelves. From the Bible's perspective, the work itself isn't the most important thing. As with most areas of your life, what really matters is what's going on in your heart.

In Colossians 3:23, we're instructed to work at whatever we do with all of our hearts *as for the Lord*. Your boss might be the greatest person ever or a real jerk, but the Bible says that shouldn't matter at the end of the day. Jesus' followers are called to work for God, not for our human employers.

Think about how radical that idea is. What if every Christian working at McDonald's or the swimming pool or a big retail store worked as if Jesus were their boss? Would they work harder? Would they do their work better? Would they think about how they spend the time he's paying them for their efforts? That's a challenging idea, but one with incredible potential.

You can always spot the employees who hate working, can't you? You can tell it by the way they do their jobs. Because it's "just" working at a retail store or a restaurant or a swimming pool or a grocery store, they treat the job like it's worthless. They don't realize the value of the skills they're developing.

Working hard is not just a matter of obedience; it also pays off in huge personal benefits. Let's take a look at some work-related wisdom from the book of Proverbs.

Do you see a man skilled in his work?
He will serve before kings;
he will not serve before obscure men."
(Proverbs 22:29)

If you become good at what you do, somebody will always want to hire you—no matter what your job is. If you're working for minimum wage—whether your job is cleaning or watching kids or answering phones—you may not feel as though you're doing anything that counts for much—at least not as far as your future career is concerned. But what you're really doing is building your customer service skills. You're figuring out what an employer wants and how to get it done. You're learning time management on the job, not to mention all kinds of other valuable skills you'll need in future jobs. Since you've agreed to sell your time for cash anyway, why not get everything you can out of the job by building whatever skills that job requires? The writer of Proverbs suggests that skillful workers tend to end up in positions of influence.

If you currently have a job, make a list of all the skills that are involved in doing that job. Ask yourself: *Am I getting good at those skills? Have I noticed an improvement in my performance?*

Diligent hands will rule,
but laziness ends in slave labor.
(Proverbs 12:24)

Speaking of influence, this proverb teaches that hard workers tend to find their way to the top. Those workers who are willing to do a good job often end up in management positions. But those who slack off when no one is looking— or who do a lousy job—often end up in less-than-desirable positions.

> Ask yourself: *Do I work hard? Do I have a reputation for doing the job right the first time? If not, how could I change that? How could I work harder or do more with my time?*

All hard work brings a profit,
but mere talk leads only to poverty.
(Proverbs 14:23)

On every job I've ever held, there's an unspoken tension about how much time the employees spend hanging out and talking. Even when I'm doing a job for myself, I'm aware of how easy it is to stop working and start yakking. My cell phone certainly doesn't help matters. The writer of Proverbs understood that tension. He knew that when the talking starts, the working stops.

Some employers don't mind their employees' talking, as long as their work still gets done. Other supervisors get frustrated by the amount of time that's "wasted" on conversation. Ask yourself: *Is this a problem on my job? Does my talking ever get in the way of the work getting done? If so, what can I do about it?*

Finish your outdoor work
and get your fields ready;
after that, build your house.
(Proverbs 24:27)

As a student, your work might include studying and doing other types of homework. Or maybe you're one of the thousands of students who are beginning to work for themselves. Either way, if you're a set-your-own-hours kind of a person, this proverb suggests a strategy: Get the work done first, then worry about providing for your "lifestyle."

The writer is speaking to people who live in a farming community. Don't worry about getting the house built if the fields aren't ready, he says. You won't have money to pay for the food to eat in your nice house if you don't do the work first. It's always a good idea to get the homework—or paying work—out of the way *before* we do the fun stuff.

I know it's tough to believe sometimes, but the work you do—and how you do it—really matters. That's because God cares more about your character and what's going on in your heart than he does about your take-home pay or the social significance of your work. Don't let low-paying jobs define you. A wise person once said, "You can either let your work determine your value—or you can reveal your value by the way you work." Even if you're earning just minimum wage, you increase your own value—and the perceived value of the God you represent—by treating your work like it matters.

Jesus reveals an important principle about work in Luke 16:1-15 (The Parable of the Shrewd Manager). Those who learn to be responsible in handling smaller responsibilities—like part-time jobs and school homework—will eventually be trusted with larger jobs. Hard work and honesty is the path to greater areas of influence—and sometimes to greater wealth.

Do you want to make the most of your time and money to find a life that matters? Start by learning to work smart and work hard at whatever you're given to do today.

CHAPTER 13
SHRED THE CREDIT CARDS!

A story on MSN's Money Web site included this quote from Andrea Alba, a 19-year-old college student: "It was fine at first. I used it mainly for gas. Then it just got deeper and deeper." Can you hear the scary music building as the monster sneaks up on the unsuspecting girl and swipes her card at the gas pump?

After she's been devoured by the beast, the story offers this quote of despair: "I just want to pay everything off," she says. "I wish I didn't have to struggle so much."

The "monster" is debt—more specifically, credit card debt. It's not unusual to hear people your parents' age saying the things this girl said. However, the debt monster has started hunting for younger victims. According to the story, Andrea already had $2,500 worth of credit card debt by her eighteenth birthday. And by age 19, she was working three jobs just to pay her credit card bills (MP Dunleavey, "How Teens Get Sucked into Credit-Card Debt").

You probably know some college students with credit cards—and credit card debt. I remember getting my first credit card offers in college and thinking, *Do these people not understand that I don't have any money?* I eventually learned that "those people" understand that fact perfectly. In fact, their plan is to be the first ones in line to ask for any money I might earn some day—if I ever get around to it.

It's no wonder that 80 percent of college students graduate with credit card debt before they get their first job. Since the college market is now saturated, the credit companies are aiming for high school students in order to catch them before they have all of their cards maxed out.

According to surveys conducted by Robert Manning, the author of *Credit Card*

*Nation: The Consequences of America's
Addiction to Credit* (Basic Books, 2000),
the number of incoming college freshmen
with credit card debt tripled between
1999 and 2002. And student lender
Nellie Mae reports those freshmen carry
an average balance of $1,585. That's
a lot of debt for an 18-year-old whose
part-time job probably pays less than
his annual tuition.

The card companies make credit look
appealing, don't they? "There are some
things money can't buy. For everything
else, there's MasterCard." They flash im-
ages of travel to exotic locations, memo-
ry-making events with friends and family, the latest fashions, and cool electron-
ics. "Don't have the cash for these must-
have experiences?" they ask. "That's
okay—charge it. We'll be there for you!"

Most of us have learned the hard way
that the credit card companies really *will*
be there for you—every month. Month

after month after month, they'll be there saying, "Please pay us." Or "Sir, your payment last month was late; that's another $40 you owe us." Or "Ma'am, because of your late payment, we're raising your interest rate to 24 percent."

Some parents contribute to the problem without realizing it. They mistakenly believe that giving their teenager a credit card helps build credit and teaches responsibility. So they co-sign the credit application for kids under 18 and send their young one out with a warning to "be careful." But it takes only a few impulsive decisions to put you behind on credit. And once you're behind a little, it's really easy to get behind a lot.

Some people have the self-control to use their credit cards sparingly and pay off their balance every month. But they're becoming the very rare exception. Credit card debt is a national epidemic. A recent study found that of all the people who file for bankruptcy, 19 percent are college students! One out of every five bankruptcies is filed by a student!

For the last two years, Americans as a whole have spent more money than we've made. In economic terms that's called a "negative savings rate." It means that as a nation, we had more going out of our pockets than coming into them. That's only happened twice before in our history—both times during the Great Depression when there were no jobs and everyone was broke. The difference now is that the economy is soaring; we're all just living on debt.

The good news is that you're young enough to avoid falling into the trap— or to climb out now. What you need is some real wisdom about credit cards. Fortunately, the Bible offers plenty of helpful guidelines.

CHAPTER 14
WISDOM PRINCIPLES

Pay your debts

God's Word makes it clear that we must always pay back what we borrow. Therefore, we should never borrow more than we can repay. To be obedient to God, we must count the cost before we borrow money. Part of the problem with credit cards is that they make it easy to borrow without thinking.

> Let no debt remain outstanding, except the continuing debt to love one another, for he who loves his fellowman has fulfilled the law. (Romans 13:8)

> The wicked borrow and do not repay, but the righteous give generously. (Psalm 37:21)

GOD PROVIDES, NOT PLASTIC

We're called to trust God completely to provide for our needs. Sometimes, however, we use our credit cards to buy things for ourselves because we're not sure God will provide us with the cash to buy them outright. Do you see the problem with that choice? Instead of waiting for God to give us something we want, we're taking it now and hoping he'll provide the money we need to pay for it later.

Some people call that "presuming" on God's grace. Instead of making our request and waiting to see if God says *yes, no,* or *wait* by providing the finances to get what we want, we simply acquire the thing and hope his answer eventually would have been yes.

God often directs our lives through our circumstances—including our finances. If I'm looking for God's will about whether I should take a backpacking trip through Europe and I realize I don't have enough money to go—and Mom and Dad aren't going to pay for it—then that very well might be God's direction not to go.

If I ask God for a new pair of shoes and I don't come up with a way to pay for those shoes, then I can consider that to be his saying no to the request—for now. If I skip that whole process and just borrow the money on my card, I don't have to worry about trusting God—until the credit card bill comes. And in the process, I may ignore the very method he would have used to show me his will.

DON'T WORRY

But what if you need food? Clothes? A place to live? The Bible doesn't forbid us from borrowing money. But it does urge us to trust God for what we need. Jesus told his followers to dump their worries about material possessions:

> "Therefore I tell you, do not worry about your life, what you will eat or drink; or about your body, what you will wear. Is not life more important than food, and the body

more important than clothes? Look at the birds of the air; they do not sow or reap or store away in barns, and yet your heavenly Father feeds them. Are you not much more valuable than they? Who of you by worrying can add a single hour to his life? And why do you worry about clothes? See how the lilies of the field grow. They do not labor or spin. Yet I tell you that not even Solomon in all his splendor was dressed like one of these. If that is how God clothes the grass of the field, which is here today and to-morrow is thrown into the fire, will he not much more clothe you, O you of little faith? So do not worry, say-ing, 'What shall we eat?' or 'What shall we drink?' or 'What shall we wear?' For the pagans run after all these things, and your heavenly Father knows that you need them." (Matthew 6:25-32)

Did you catch what Jesus said there? God knows what we need. He's tuned in to our lives. He cares about what we care about. God promises to provide what we need. We can trust him.

I can hear some of you saying, "I know God provides what I *need*. It's the stuff I *want* that I'm worried about—the good stuff that I'd like to have, but I'm afraid he won't give it to me. That's why I need credit cards."

GOD LIKES TO GIVE US COOL STUFF

Take a look at Jesus' words in Matthew 7:9-11—

> Which of you, if his son asks for bread, will give him a stone? Or if he asks for a fish, will give him a snake? If you, then, though you are evil, know how to give good gifts to your children, how much more will your Father in heaven

give good gifts to those who ask
him!

God loves to give good gifts to his children. I have to admit—I understood
this passage much better after I became
a dad. Very few things make me hap-
pier than giving something to my kids
that I know they'll love. I love to watch
their eyes light up when I pull out a
special gift. Their excitement makes me
feel great because I love my kids. How
much more does our Father in heaven
love us?

James 1:17 tells us that every good
gift we've ever received came from one
place—our Father in heaven. If you
make a list of all the good things that
have ever come your way, you'll run out
of ink before you run out of things to
list. The original source of every good
thing is God, no matter how it makes
its way into our lives.

What's that got to do with credit card

debt? Only this—if you want something and God hasn't provided a way for you to get it yet (without overextending your credit card), maybe the thing you want isn't good for you right now. If it *is* good, God will provide it. You can trust him.

LENDERS OWN YOU

Sometimes we can't avoid borrowing money. But making the choice to swipe your credit card always comes with a very high price:

> The rich rule over the poor, and the borrower is servant to the lender. (Proverbs 22:7)

We become servants of anyone to whom we owe money. In a very real way, borrowing money is about selling our freedom. The companies and people who hold our loans become our masters. We have to keep working because, in a sense, we belong to them until the money is paid back. Being in debt—especially credit card debt—should always make us a little uncomfortable for that reason.

SCENARIO: TAKING WHAT'S MINE?

Maria knew Jake was a Christian. They'd had several late-night talks about God, Jesus, and heaven while they were closing up the restaurant. Jake had been praying for months that Maria would come to know Jesus as her Savior. Maria seemed interested in the things Jake told her, but two things bothered her.

The first had to do with preachers on TV who asked people to send them money and promised blessings and riches in return. Maria's grandmother lived on a very tight budget, but she was always sending $20 to one preacher or another. Maria thought they were taking advantage of her grandmother, and Jake mostly agreed with her.

The second obstacle was that Maria had seen Jake being sneaky with money. At their restaurant all of the wait staff were supposed to put their tips into one big jar and then divide it up equally at the end of the night. The guy who trained Jake had said that he thought the rule was stupid and that everyone pocketed a buck or two out of most tips and put the rest of their money into the jar. So Jake followed his trainer's example. It made sense to him because he worked hard for those tips. He took good care of his customers, and he often got bigger tips because of it. Sometimes his regulars even said to him, "Now this is just for you; you don't have to share it." Jake agreed.

But when Maria asked him about it, Jake realized he'd been rationalizing his decision to keep part of his tips for himself. He knew what the rules were when he took the job. The fact that a few other guys broke them didn't make it okay for him to do so. He realized he'd actually been stealing from Maria, in a way. He hated that Maria was disappointed in him, and even worse—he hated that she might lump him in with other so-called Christians who cared more about money than anything else.

THINK ABOUT:

· Was Maria right? Was Jake stealing? Was he being unethical?

· Have you ever been in a situation like Jake's?

· If Jake was wrong, what should he do? How can he make it right with Maria and the rest of the wait staff?

· What has his dishonesty cost him?

· What has it potentially cost Maria?

· What will it cost Jake to come clean?

THINK AHEAD:

· How does the way we deal with money and financial situations reveal our character?

· Is it ever okay not to tell the whole truth about money?

· Do you sometimes have to be a little sneaky to get what's yours? Why or why not?

· How much money are integrity and a clean conscience worth?

CHAPTER 15

YOUR MONEY OR
YOUR CHARACTER?

The apostle Peter said Christians should "live such good lives among the pagans that, though they accuse you of doing wrong, they may see your good deeds and glorify God on the day he visits us" (1 Peter 2:12). That wise direction applies to money as much as anything else.

Proverbs 22:1 backs up that notion: "A good name is more desirable than great riches; to be esteemed is better than silver or gold." Solomon taught that a person's reputation is worth far more than any amount of money. And when you represent Jesus, your rep counts for even more.

Money is typically the area where most people cut corners on their integrity. John the Baptist understood that. When a group of people came to him and asked what they should do to clean up their lives before God, his answers had a lot to do with being honest about money:

> "What should we do then?" the crowd asked.
>
> John answered, "The man with two tunics should share with him who has none, and the one who has food should do the same."
>
> Tax collectors also came to be baptized. "Teacher," they asked, "what should we do?"
>
> "Don't collect any more than you are required to," he told them.
>
> Then some soldiers asked him, "And what should we do?"
>
> He replied, "Don't extort money and don't accuse people falsely— be content with your pay." (Luke 3:10-14)

That last one can be tough: "Be content with your pay." A lack of contentment about how much money we have is what leads us to compromise our integrity. We need to be honest with ourselves and admit that cheating with money is the same as lying. And God hates lying: "The Lord abhors dishonest scales, but accurate weights are his delight" (Proverbs 11:1).

A "dishonest scale" is one set to read the weight as more than it really is. A dishonest butcher might set his scale to read a little heavy in order to make a tiny bit more money on each sale. A gas station owner could do the same by setting the pump to count less than a gallon of gas as a full gallon.

God "abhors" (hates) when people lie about money. And he makes sure they feel the effects of their lies.

Food gained by fraud tastes sweet
to a man, but he ends up with

a mouth full of gravel. (Proverbs 20:17)

Why would someone try to cheat his coworkers out of cash? Why would someone lie about how much work she did just to get paid a little extra? Why would someone disobey Jesus' command to pay taxes by not reporting how much he made?

The answer is greed—the desire for more and more money. Greed springs from the fear that God won't meet all of our needs. Or he won't give us all we want. We lie about money because we prefer to *get* more rather than *trust* God more.

Bottom line: It's never wise to lie, cheat, or steal for the sake of money. Whatever financial gains you make are wiped out by the damage you cause to your reputation and to your relationship with God.

SCENARIO: TOO BROKE TO GIVE

When Emily got her first paycheck from her new job at the bank, she was excited. She'd been cruising the Web sites of a few of her favorite stores for some shoes, and she also wanted to get a couple of new CDs. But when she looked at her check, she was shocked by how small her take-home pay was. She hadn't realized how much her employer would hold back for taxes.

She started thinking about the things she'd have to pay for with her check: car insurance, gas, and her upcoming mission trip. When she added it all up, she realized she'd have hardly any money left over. And when Emily mentioned it to her mom, her mom had the nerve to say, "Don't forget to give some of it back to God."

Ugh. Emily had forgotten about putting some of her check into the offering. And now that she'd mentally spent all of her money, she didn't really feel like giving up any more of it. Why did her church need her money when so many adults with full-time jobs were already giving? Maybe she could wait until she was out of college to start giving to her church.

THINK ABOUT:

· Have you ever wondered the same things that Emily wondered?

· Do you think it's your responsibility to give some of your money to your church or to other good causes? Why or why not?

· Is everyone required to give some of his/her money back to God?

· Should giving be left up to fully-employed adults?

· What will it cost Emily to give away part of her small income?

· What will it cost her to keep it all for herself?

· Should she include paying for her mission trip as part of her giving to church? Why or why not?

THINK AHEAD:

· How do you really feel about giving some of your hard-earned dollars to your church? Why do you feel that way?

· Do you think your heart can be changed for the better? For the worse?

· Does God need our cash?

· Does God like us less if we don't give?

· What are the benefits of being generous with our money?

CHAPTER 16
GIVE IT AWAY!

The first thing you need to understand about giving is that it has little to do with whether or not your church—or a missionary or a pregnancy center—needs your money. Like everything else we've talked about regarding money, our giving has to do with our hearts. Do we really believe God is the source of our income? Are we convinced we can trust him to take care of us? Do we understand that when we give away money, we're joining God in his work to take care of the poor, protect the innocent, and spread his truth around the world?

Being generous with our money shows we're not afraid that God's going to start holding back on us. It shows we're not worried that we're going to lose out by letting go of what's ours. It shows we trust him more than we trust our dough.

There's a funny thing about becoming generous people. Yes, it's sometimes hard to give; everyone has experienced that hesitation. But it's also hard to give without getting a lot back.

GENEROSITY PAYS!

Several Bible passages confirm that giving away what's ours to give tends to bring blessing back to us.

> A generous man will prosper; he who refreshes others will himself be refreshed. (Proverbs 11:25)

> They are always generous and lend freely; their children will be blessed. (Psalm 37:26)

> Good will come to him who is generous and lends freely. (Psalm 112:5)

> A generous man will himself be blessed, for he shares his food with the poor. (Proverbs 22:9)

> Remember this: Whoever sows sparingly will also reap sparingly, and whoever sows generously will also reap generously. (2 Corinthians 9:6)

These verses don't necessarily mean that if you put $20 in the offering plate on Sunday morning, you'll find $20 in your pocket on Monday. But we can assume two things:

First, generous people get treated generously. The fact is that we like to do things for people who like to do things for us. If I'm known as the guy who's there to help by offering my time and money where it's needed, then it makes sense that others will want to help me whenever I'm stuck.

Second, God loves it when we imitate his character—and he's the most generous giver of all. If we demonstrate a willingness to help others, he'll give us more opportunities to do it—with more resources.

Of course, giving wisely involves more than just bursts of occasional generosity; it requires a plan of action.

GIVE A PERCENTAGE

Christians sometimes argue with each other about whether or not the Bible requires us to give a "tithe"—that is, a tenth of all our income. I won't make a case for either side, other than to say that the clear example in God's Word is that Christians should regularly give some percentage of their income back to God.

In Genesis 14, Abraham gave a tithe to a mysterious priest named Melchizedek. Later, giving a portion of one's income became part of the Law of Moses. Finally, we see the practice confirmed by Paul in his instructions to the Corinthians about their planned gifts for the financial needs of others:

> On the first day of every week, each one of you should set aside a sum of money in keeping with his income, saving it up, so that when I come no collections will have to be made. (1 Corinthians 16:2)

The wisdom of Scripture suggests that we should regularly give a percentage, "in keeping with our income," back to the Lord. What percentage? Ten percent is the figure mentioned most often in the Old Testament. In truth, many people gave far greater percentages than that. Unfortunately, many Christians today give far less than 10 percent.

When Jesus talked about giving, he reserved his praise not for the biggest givers, but for the person who gave the largest percentage of her income—all of it. You'll find the story in Luke 21:1-4. A widow who had only two copper coins to her name gave them both to the temple. She had nothing left. Apparently, she trusted God to provide for her needs. Jesus pointed out that everyone else gave "out of their wealth," a tiny portion of their income when compared to the widow's 100 percent.

Ask God to work in your heart to help you come to an understanding of what percentage of your income you should give back to him. Be honest with yourself. And be willing to sacrifice and trust him to meet your needs.

GIVE WHAT YOU'VE AGREED ON—AND ENJOY IT

Once you've agreed to give God a certain percentage of your income, your job is to keep that promise—and to have fun fulfilling it:

Each man should give what he has decided in his heart to give, not reluctantly or under compulsion, for God loves a cheerful giver. (2 Corinthians 9:7)

Actually, the word for *cheerful* in the original language might also be translated *hilarious*. God loves it when we love giving to him. Putting money in the plate at church or giving to an organization that helps the poor is not like paying taxes. It should not be done with anger or reluctance. God isn't making us give up our money. He's allowing us to contribute to his work in the world through our gifts of time and money.

It's an honor to be able to give money back to God. If we don't enjoy it, it might be time to ask what's going on in our hearts. What matters most to us—following God or getting what's coming to us? It's not an easy question to answer.

GIVE FOR HIS GLORY, NOT YOURS

During the offering at church, you can always tell when the plate goes by a little kid whose mom or dad gave him some money to contribute. You can hear the clink and clang of the pennies, dimes, and nickels all over the church.

That's a good thing; those kids are learning to give. But some of us wish we could keep getting that kind of attention with our giving later in life. "Look how much I gave, everyone! See how spiritual I am! Yay, me!"

Jesus addresses that attitude in Matthew 6:2-4:

> "So when you give to the needy, do not announce it with trumpets, as the hypocrites do in the synagogues

and on the streets, to be honored by men. I tell you the truth, they have received their reward in full. But when you give to the needy, do not let your left hand know what your right hand is doing, so that your giving may be in secret. Then your Father, who sees what is done in secret, will reward you."

Don't tell people how much you put in the plate, how much you sent to Compassion International, or how much you gave to a friend in a tough spot. Politicians who are running for office will do that to earn points with voters. The only voter who should matter to you is God.

GIVE PERSONALLY

In addition to giving back to God out of a spirit of obedience, part of our motivation should be gratitude for all of God's goodness to us. Giving is part of our worship of our generous Creator, Redeemer, and Father.

A woman named Mary understood that motivation. On the night before the Last Supper, she took an extremely expensive perfume—a jar worth a year's wages—broke it, and poured the whole thing on Jesus' hair and feet. Then she dried his feet with her long hair.

This act of worship was costly and not exactly practical. Judas grumbled that the jar could have been sold and the money used to feed a lot of poor people. Of course, Judas was a thief, so his motive wasn't pure. But he had a point—until Jesus replied to his complaint:

> "Leave her alone," said Jesus. "Why are you bothering her? She has done a beautiful thing to me. The poor you will always have with you, and you can help them any time you want. But you will

not always have me. She did what she could. She poured perfume on my body beforehand to prepare for my burial. I tell you the truth, wherever the gospel is preached throughout the world, what she has done will also be told, in memory of her." (Mark 14:6-9)

Mary gave an expensive, impractical gift of time (a year's worth of work) and money, but she didn't just sell it on eBay and deposit the check in Jesus' bank account. Instead, directed by God, she gave her gift to prepare Jesus for his burial. She responded to Jesus' need, and she found a beautiful way to contribute.

Most students don't have a lot of money to give, but God wants your *heart* most of all. Is he calling you to offer yourself in some beautiful, extravagant, impractical way that will help make Christ known to the world around you? Are you listening to find out what that way is?

CHAPTER 17
USING WEALTH WISELY

If you've been jumping around in this book and have now arrived at the last bit, then you might believe that God wants us all to be poor, that he doesn't want us to have anything cool, or that having wealth means we're bad Christians. I hope that's not the conclusion you've reached. The Bible doesn't teach that.

What it does teach is that time and money are tools—two things we can use to accomplish God's will in our lives and in the world around us.

BUILDING WEALTH

The best way to acquire wealth so it's available for us to use for God's glory is to save and invest what we earn. Would it surprise you to learn that the book of Proverbs offers some wisdom on how to do that?

Dishonest money dwindles away, but he who gathers money little by little makes it grow. (Proverbs 13:11)

If you want to have money to use for good and to enjoy as a gift from God, you have to learn to set it aside "little by little." Very few people strike it rich in business or win the lottery. Most wealthy people get where they are by saving a little at a time and by putting their money to work through reliable investments.

Many smart parents try to instill in their kids an understanding of the importance of saving. When a friend of mine was really young, he received a dollar every week from his parents. They'd give him ten dimes, but they'd stack eight of them and say, "This is yours to spend however you want." Next they'd set one dime next to the stack and say, "This is yours to give back to God by putting it in the offering plate." And then they'd take the final dime and say, "This is yours to put in your piggy bank to save for something big."

That's a great financial lesson, no matter how old you are. Whenever you get a check, immediately set aside the percentage you've agreed to give to God. Set aside another percentage (perhaps 10 percent) to save for the future. And then enjoy spending the rest of it with a clear conscience. If you make this practice a habit now—as a student—you'll be absolutely amazed at how much money you can save over the next several years. And if you let that money "ride" on into your 20s and 30s, then you'll find yourself miles ahead of most of your friends.

BEING SHREWD

Jesus once told a story in which he seemed to praise a character who did something really unethical. Honest! Take a look for yourself:

> Jesus told his disciples: "There was a rich man whose manager was accused of wasting his possessions. So he called him in and asked him, 'What is this I hear about you? Give an account of your management, because you cannot be manager any longer.'
>
> "The manager said to himself, 'What shall I do now? My master is taking away my job. I'm not strong enough to dig, and I'm ashamed to beg—I know what I'll do so that, when I lose my job here, people will welcome me into their houses.'
>
> "So he called in each one of his master's debtors. He asked the first, 'How much do you owe my master?'

" 'Eight hundred gallons of olive oil,' he replied.

"The manager told him, 'Take your bill, sit down quickly, and make it four hundred.'

"Then he asked the second, 'And how much do you owe?'

" 'A thousand bushels of wheat,' he replied.

"He told him, 'Take your bill and make it eight hundred.'

"The master commended the dishonest manager because he had acted shrewdly. For the people of this world are more shrewd in dealing with their own kind than are the people of the light. I tell you, use worldly wealth to gain friends for yourselves, so that when it is gone, you will be welcomed into eternal dwellings." (Luke 16:1-9)

Okay, Jesus didn't exactly praise the guy for his unethical actions, but he did praise him for using money as a helpful tool in his relationships. Jesus told the story to make the point that wealth can be used for eternal purposes. He wants those of us who end up with some wealth to use it shrewdly to influence people and build God's kingdom. Money, when it's gained in the right way and used with wisdom, can be an awesome device to spread the good news of Jesus.

In another New Testament passage, Paul gave Timothy a message to pass on to people who had great wealth. What's interesting is that Paul didn't repeat the command Jesus gave to the rich young ruler (to sell everything and give the money to the poor). Instead, Paul instructed people of wealth to put their hope in God alone, to enjoy every good thing in their lives as a gift from God, and to use their resources to help others as a way of investing in the life that really matters.

> Command them to do good, to be rich in good deeds, and to be generous and willing to share. In this way they will lay up treasure for themselves as a firm foundation for the coming age, so that they may take hold of the life that is truly life. (1 Timothy 6:18-19)

God clearly doesn't oppose the idea of rich Christians. When you think about it, by any global measure, most believers in the Western world are rich Christians. So these commands to use our wealth to do good, to share with others, and to build wealth in heaven apply to most of us.

Wisdom, self-control, and good planning are the keys to building wealth. Proverbs 21:20 describes it this way: "In the house of the wise are stores of choice food and oil, but a foolish man devours all he has."

I know of a church that stored up a lot of food and supplies back at the turn of the millennium when some people thought Y2K was going to bring disaster. Just to be safe, church members wanted to have stores available to help those in need. The church's plan required forward thinking, money, and self-control. Even though the whole Y2K thing turned out to be just a lot of hype, I admired the way these church members thought ahead. I admired even more the *reason why* they thought ahead—to use material things (wealth) to help the poor and influence people with the good news about Jesus.

Don't be afraid to start financially storing up for yourself today. Wisdom demands it. Just be ready and willing to share what you have when God gives you the opportunity to do so.

CHAPTER 18
FINAL THOUGHT

Thanks for reading this little book about finding wisdom on time and money. I hope you remember a few important things:

1. All worthwhile wisdom comes from God. He offers it free to all who ask for it, and he loves for us to look for it in the pages of his Word.

2. God gives everyone resources. Most of us have a little money of our own, and all of us have time. Those resources are given to us as gifts to use for God's glory.

3. In order to make the best use of our resources, we must be willing to sacrifice our lives to follow Jesus. Unless we start there, all the management tools in the world won't help us use our time and money in ways that really matter.

4. Everyone makes mistakes with time and money. Don't look back in regret. Get wisdom and ask God for the courage to make wiser choices next time. You can do this; he will help you. Go for it!